ANDREW DOW

Christianity Unwrapped

God's Rescue Pack Revealed

LITTLE HOUSE IN

- JOPPA -

Christianity if false is of no importance, and if true, of infinite importance. The one thing it cannot be is moderately important.

C.S. Lewis

Contents

Preface

Dear Reader

The year 2023 will mark the 52nd anniversary of my ordination into the ministry of the Church of England, so, yes, I've been a "Rev" for over half a century! During that time, whilst preaching about the claims of Christ to be the Lord and Saviour of the world, I would often challenge people to make a simple commitment to him, using a prayer similar to the one you will find at the end of this book. If someone spoke to me at the end of the service indicating that they had "clinched" it with Jesus in that way, I would offer them one of a number of short booklets or tracts available from established church sources. These were entirely fit for purpose, but I longed to be in a position to give them something more personal, in other words written by me! So I definitely had "a book in me", but given the pressures of parish ministry, no real time or space to put pen to paper.

That all changed with retirement, and in particular the enforced inactivity of the Covid lockdowns. So 'Christianity Unwrapped' first appeared in 2021. I've been delighted to give or sell copies quite widely, and to see it used by several church home groups in different locations. (*Some of those groups have found this book's appendix helpful, with its comprehensive extra notes, Bible references, and questions for discussion.*)

I thoroughly enjoyed writing 'Christianity Unwrapped', and I believe it contains stimulating and challenging material for a wide variety of people. So are you an open-minded sceptic? Then turn to the earlier chapters, where through the interventions of a persistent invisible 'heckler', (printed in italics) I raise arguments frequently used against Christianity, and then attempt to rebut them! Or perhaps you would call yourself an honest doubter? Did Jesus really exist, let alone rise from the dead?! I try to give well-reasoned answers to these questions, in sections which would be technically called 'apologetics'. Or maybe you are a new Christian – you have only recently decided to follow Jesus – and there's lots in the Bible you don't yet know or understand. Well, you will find in Chapter 4 details of seven of the stupendous claims Jesus made for himself, as well as explanations of some of the Bible's mega words or themes, such as 'incarnation', 'grace', 'sin', 'reconciliation', the 'Holy Spirit'.

Finally, I would like to thank my wife, Miriam, and my daughters, Jennie and Carrie, for their unstinting support and encouragement down the years; and also to express my appreciation to a number of trusted Christian friends who read through earlier drafts of 'Christianity Unwrapped', before offering helpful alternative wordings. In addition, I would like to thank my sister-in-law, Rosemary Cragg, for her careful proof reading, and my friend, Martin Skellern for his invaluable assistance in getting my book published in this form.

I hope and pray that reading 'Christianity Unwrapped' will draw you into a personal knowledge of Jesus Christ as your Saviour, Ruler, and 'Friend', or strengthen your faith in him if you are already committed. Do contact me at the above address if I can be of further help.

Andrew Dow

Moreton-in-Marsh, January 2023

andrewdow451@btinternet.com

Introduction

C hristianity ..... **unwrapped?** Why does it need to be?

The rise in popular atheism and agnosticism, public impatience with traditional religion, and the Church's high- profile failures have combined to push the Christian Faith 'under wraps', forgotten, marginalised and misunderstood, ridiculed even. This book is an attempt to 'take off the coverings', revealing again the wonder and power of God's rescue act in Christ.

Down the centuries, there have been countless religions, philosophies, and 'isms' that have enjoyed their heyday, only to be consigned to the ideological trash. So why in this 21ˢᵗ century should Christianity be freshly massaged in the way you propose?

Because all the religions of the world seek to meet the spiritual aspirations of a single human race, they will share some common features, the practice of prayer for example. More specifically, Judaism, Christianity and Islam are united in their passionate assertion, in the face of polytheism, that there is only one God. However, the Christian Faith is worthy of special attention because on its arrival it offered to the world, and still

1

does, three fresh and priceless perspectives:

1. A unique portrait of God, his nature and character
2. A unique narrative of God's actions on behalf of humankind
3. A radically new ethic, or code of conduct

You're assuming, of course, that God exists; but hasn't modern science disproved all that?

It depends what you mean by 'proof'. We can prove mathematically that $2 + 2 = 4$, but there are some things that really matter that cannot be decisively proved in that way. We cannot prove, for instance, that our mothers love us. I can present plenty of evidence of my mother's love, but you could undermine any so-called proof I offer by saying, "She is pretending, because she wants your money or hopes that you will look after her in her old age." In the same way, despite what might be called compelling probabilities, or evidence, the atheist cannot prove there is no God, just as the believer cannot prove that there is. All that each can do is to examine the same available evidence, and come to their own conclusions, albeit diametric opposites! In that sense, both atheist and believer are exercising a measure of faith; both are living by faith in their ability correctly to interpret the data. So don't let the atheist lay any claim to the intellectual high ground in this debate - unbeliever and believer compete here on level territory! No surprise, therefore, that there are many highly intelligent and gifted scientists who are also deeply committed Christians.

A friend of mine, speaking in support of the existence of God at a school sixth-form debate, won the final vote with what turned out to be the knock-out punch: "There are a number of unbelievable things," he said (with a wry smile on his face), "that an unbeliever must continue to believe, in order to remain an unbeliever."(!) "The first," he said, as the teenagers shifted uneasily in their seats, "is to believe that this amazing universe in which we live came into being by chance, rather than by design."

"So consider our planet, the Earth, and its distance from the sun. A little further away, and we'd freeze. A tiny bit closer, and we'd fry. It is, quite literally, in-credible to think that such precise spacing, crucial to human existence and survival, was the result of some cosmic accident."

My friend could have gone on from creation to conscience. Once a human child has learned how to put a sentence together, what are the first words almost universally uttered? Answer: "That's not fair!" A burning sense of perceived injustice from the lips of babes and sucklings! Where has that come from? Merely from some genetically driven social programming down the generations, as unbelievers are compelled to…err…believe? Or has this concept of justice been hard wired into every human life - by the moral, righteous creative Force that rational believers call 'God'?

Then there is the 'Jesus phenomenon', the extraordinary, itinerant preacher from Nazareth. By any reckoning, religious or secular, he has stood as a giant colossus astride the centuries-wide expanse of history. His profound teaching, peerless example, powerful healings, prophetic leadership and heartfelt compassion - where did it all come from, if not sourced and turbo-charged, as Jesus himself claimed, by his personal, prayerful filial relationship with God, the one he called 'Father'? "The Father and I are one," Jesus said, "I always do what the Father wills."

So can it be credible that Jesus was wrong on this crucial point; that he was mistaken, misled, deluded even, about the existence of God? It simply doesn't add up, but it's on that shaky notion that atheists must rest their faith.

All right, I'll let your "God" go through – for now. You may proceed with your 'unwrapping'!

Christianity offers a unique portrait of God

Christianity's roots are to be found in Judaism - Jesus was a Jew - so it's no surprise that all the attributes of God portrayed in the Jewish Scriptures (what our Bibles call the Old Testament) are reaffirmed in the specifically Christian part of the Bible, the New Testament. So Jesus believed, as his forbears had done, in one God, the sole Creator God; a God who was all-glorious and powerful, all-seeing, all-knowing, the Sovereign Lord of all nations, a righteous God totally committed to justice for "the last, the lost, and the least"; and, supremely, a God who was loving and full of compassion. There is a popular notion that the God of the Old Testament displays only wrath, and the God of the New only love. Don't believe a word of it! Search the Gospels (the four biographies we have of Jesus), and you will discover Jesus (tear-stained?) speaking more of the danger of Hell than the promise of Heaven. Examine the Old Testament thoroughly, and you will encounter a God whose tender compassionate care for his 'offspring' betrays all the marks of a deeply doting parent! (Hosea, chapter 11, verses 1-4; Isaiah, chapter 49, verse 15)

And it is this very special characteristic of God that Jesus of Nazareth uniquely and powerfully brought onto the world stage. "When you pray," he once memorably taught, "say 'Our Father in heaven'", the opening phrase of what Christians call 'the Lord's Prayer' (St Matthew, chapter 6, verse 9). Talk to God as if he were your father, with respect or reverence, but with intimacy, because you know he loves you.

To Jesus' Jewish listeners, this would have been arresting, but as we've seen from the Old Testament, not entirely without ancient precedent. To the Romans, Greeks and other Gentiles inhabiting the Mediterranean basin, however, it would have been astonishing, almost ludicrous. A father-like god, motherly even, a god who loves? What a contrast to our Pantheon to which we pay grudging lip service, zeus@mountolympus.org, that cartel of fickle, for ever in- fighting, untrustworthy deities!

My father was a poor role model, so this concept is a problem for me.

No earthly parents get it right all the time. Jesus obviously has in mind the ideal father figure: someone who consistently and patiently cares for his children, comforts them, counsels

5

them, and occasionally corrects them! Jesus himself 'fathered' his followers in these ways, thereby modelling to them the love of their heavenly Father.

Isn't it then just as I thought: the Christian God is merely a crutch for the weak to lean on?

A Christian's trust in God as their Heavenly Father is about so much more than a feel-good factor. It's about a forceful hope and purpose in a world that can seem directionless and empty. So different from the atheist's bleak perspective, as expressed shortly before his death by the famous scientist, Professor Stephen Hawking: "We are insignificant creatures on a minor planet of a very average star in the outer suburbs of one of a hundred thousand million galaxies. So it is difficult to believe in a God that would care about us or even notice our existence." Agreed, very difficult, without the life and teachings of Jesus!

I've read that Muslims reject the idea of God as a Father.

The Muslim's holy book, the Koran, ascribes ninety-nine names to God, or Allah, but 'Father' is not one of them. They believe that to speak of God in such human or personal terms dishonours him; it diminishes him by lowering him to our level. The Christian, however, celebrates the very opposite: God is indeed transcendent, almighty, wrapped in unapproachable majesty; and yet as our heavenly Father, he is 'big' enough to stoop tenderly to embrace his beloved children. Jesus' God, at one and the same time, the Most High, and the Most Nigh, or Near! This divine paradox doesn't demean God; it exalts him, and becomes a wonderful revelation to a weary world!

So the Christian Faith presented the divine in a totally fresh light, but a struggling humanity needed to know not only God's true identity, but also his activity. What had this 'heavenly Father' done to demonstrate his fatherly love? Which brings us to the second of Christianity's invaluable perspectives:

Christianity offers a unique narrative of God's actions

A few years ago the mayor of Chicago spent a day disguised as a tramp living on the city's streets with the homeless. A local paper, the Chicago Tribune, described this act as "the world's greatest stoop". They were misinformed! The world's greatest stoop had occurred many centuries earlier, when God the Creator visited the world he had made. Christians call this event 'the Incarnation', literally the 'in, or into flesh', when God adopted our human form, in the person of Jesus of Nazareth. Out of his great love, the 'heavenly Father' didn't send an e-mail, or set up a zoom meeting, he just – came.

But can we be sure Jesus really existed? An entry under 'Jesus' in a communist-backed Russian dictionary runs: 'a mythical figure who never existed.'

What we know about Jesus comes from four biographies commonly called the Gospels. Entitled the Gospels of Matthew,

Mark, Luke and John, all four were written and in circulation by the end of the 1st century CE, and probably much earlier, one, St Mark, as early as 65CE. If Jesus died in about 33CE, as strongly suggested by other non-biblical sources, then St Mark's story was written a mere thirty years after the event. That is the equivalent of a historian in 2020 recalling the 1990s, a time scale with no scope for fiction, and, any make-believe wide open to speedy exposure.

Most scholars accept an early church tradition that St Mark's account is actually the memoires of Jesus' close friend, Peter, so the recollections of a first-hand eyewitness. Matthew and John were also disciples - they wrote what they saw; they described what they heard! The Bible is not the only ancient text referring to Jesus. The Roman author, Tacitus, writing in about 110CE, refers to a "Christus… executed by Pontius Pilate when Tiberius was emperor." The Gospels concur! Similarly, a contemporary Jewish historian, Josephus, writes of "one Jesus, a doer of marvellous deeds, the so-called Christ." Certainly not a Christian himself, Josephus nevertheless even mentions a rumour about this Jesus' resurrection!

So, moved by his fatherly love, God came to earth in the person of Jesus, a well-documented historical figure. However, this wasn't simply God pouring his Spirit into an ordinary human being, specially selected. It was more, far more! Truly to understand the wonder of the Incarnation, we need to retrace our steps a little, back into the Jewish scriptures. Fiercely monotheistic, certainly, but even there in the Old Testament there are hints that the one and only God is not a monolith, but can present in unique plurality. So in the Bible's account of creation, when God comes to the dramatic moment of creating humankind, he says, "Let *us* make man in our image." (Genesis, chapter 1, verse 26) *Us* - a use of the 'royal we'? What the Old Testament suggests, the New makes explicit: God is one, but 'trinitarian', a community of three in one and one in three. To think of the Godhead as being 'in community' would prove hugely significant in the future, as authentic Christianity spurned the 'I and my' of Western individualism, in favour of the 'we and us' of Semitic and African culture.

Down the centuries Christians have struggled to find homely illustrations to explain the Trinity. All fall short in some degree, because the Trinity is a divine mystery, basically inexplicable and beyond the reach of any human mind! Try this though, from the world of musical concertos where we can picture 'three-in-one' or a 'tri-unity', a trinity! Firstly, there is the conductor, in control of it all, the 'Father' of it all. Then there is the soloist bringing to life, or 'incarnating', the main thread and meaning of the music. A metaphor for Jesus, God's Son, visible on earth? And finally, there are the multiple members of the orchestra, spread over the entire stage. The Christian equivalent is the Holy Spirit, with his manifold gifts bringing it all to life. Three separate entities, yet one entity, one performance.

Very early on in the history of the Christian Faith, believers began to realise that, similarly, they could experience God unreservedly as one, but also as the Father creator, Jesus the Son, Rescuer or Saviour, and the Holy Spirit, Life Giver and In-dweller: the Christian Trinity, or triune God. Muslims strongly reject this idea (the doctrine of three gods, as they call it), pointing out that the word 'Trinity' nowhere occurs in the Christian's Bible. They are right, it doesn't, but the concept is certainly there, not as a piece of dry theological dogma, but a heart-warming expression of the three different ways in which God could be known. It's a bit like the chemical element Hydrogen Oxide, or H_2O. We can experience it in three different ways, as water, steam, or ice, but they are all fundamentally H_2O!

So when God set about the Incarnation, what was the Trinity 'doing'? The Bible's answer should take our breath away. The Father's 'Son' agreed to exchange his Father's glorious presence for residence on earth, as the only way of saving humankind. Our well-loved Christmas carols say it all: "He (Jesus) came down to earth from heaven, who is God and Lord of all", verse 2 of "Once in Royal David's City." (Why the Trinity were moved to tear themselves apart in this way we shall consider later on in the book.) The infant Jesus' divine origin explains why his conception in his mother's womb was unique, the supernatural event sometimes called the 'Virgin Birth'. Mary's egg was not fertilised by Joseph's sperm, but by the miraculous and unprecedented work of God's Spirit, "the power of the Most High", as St Luke records it. (St Luke, chapter 1, verse 35)

The Son's unprecedented move away was not a piece of altruistic downsizing; it was a total, voluntary humiliation! Consider what happened, the Christmas story as we call it. The Son arrived on earth neither in glittering Rome, nor in glorious Athens, but in gritty Bethlehem, a one-horse town in Judea, an obscure and despised Eastern outpost of the Empire. Born to wealthy and influential parents, as might befit a divine visitor, he was not. The very opposite in fact: Jesus' earthly father and mother, Joseph and Mary, were from a poor, humble, artisan family. At a stroke, God Incarnate had turned the world's values upside down, an unmistakable signal that Jesus' message would be radical, not to say revolutionary, cutting right through human pomp and pride. All this is remarkable enough, but we've yet to touch on the heart of the matter: Jesus the Son of God stooped so low, as to become – a baby! A vulnerable, totally dependent infant, "mewling and puking in the nurse's arms", as Shakespeare so delicately puts it ('As You Like It', Act 5). Except that there was no nurse on hand, as far as we can tell. Mary and Joseph were on their own; Bethlehem was far from their home in Nazareth, and the town so crowded and short of guest accommodation that Mary had to give birth, not in some normal sleeping quarters, but in a cowshed lent as a rudimentary nursery. (You can read the story in St Luke, chapter 2.)

Becoming a baby, such a humbling start for the Son of God on earth, but such a powerful message in the process! A former Archbishop of Canterbury, George Carey, hits the spot when he writes, "It's as if God slaps a price tag on our lives, a price tag which states 'beyond price' or 'priceless'." The Incarnation spells it out loud and clear: every human life, however fragile, and regardless of age, race, colour, achievement, wealth or status matters to God, a crucial viewpoint that under-girded Christianity's subsequent mission and value statements.

Contrast atheist Richard Dawkins' brutally mechanistic evaluation of the human species' worth: "The universe is nothing but a collection of atoms in motion, human beings are merely machines for propagating DNA, and the propagation of DNA is a self-sustaining process. It is every living object's sole reason for living."

Scientific humanism? De-humanism more like, not to say in-humanism; and such a viewpoint can have blood-curdling consequences. A fourteen-year-old boy at our local school, having decided that he was going to be an atheist, penned this cool exposé: "It became an emotional relief because no matter how many people's lives I ruin, it doesn't matter because they have no purpose anyway." One can only tremble at the possible life trajectory of this young man.

There remains an important question about the Incarnation. Why in order to rescue us did God have to lower himself so drastically? Could he not have parachuted in like Superman?

A simple story may provide a clue. One bitterly cold winter's day, a woman at her downstairs window watched a young bird close by vainly trying to forage some food from the frozen ground. Frantically hungry, the bird eventually hit the window's glass, injuring itself. The woman stepped outside attempting to nurse the bird, but every time she approached, it hopped feebly away, wary and frightened. How could she possibly get close enough to offer the tender shelter of her hands? And then the penny dropped, after a fashion! Fantastical though it might seem, the only real solution was for her to become a bird herself, and not just any bird, but a similar species, preferably the identical species, a partner in size, form and colour.

In just the same way, God had to identify with us in every way, beginning with infancy, sharing our world and showing our worth. Furthermore, he would have to experience more of our human condition in the raw.

And so he did. One night, when only about two years old, his parents bundled him up and fled southwards to Egypt to escape King Herod's infanticide. Jesus had joined the saddest of the world's multitudes, the multitude of refugees; and there would be more, many more, privations and dangers to come.

In 2003, the world was swept by a coronavirus, not Covid-19, but SARS (Severe Acute Respiratory Syndrome). Pupils returning from the Far East to their English boarding school had to go into quarantine for at least a week. For the whole time, their headmistress voluntarily joined them in the isolation boarding house, to show her love and concern for them, an act of solidarity to identify with them in their hour of need, a Jesus-type act.

The New Testament has a single word by way of a summary. It's the word **grace**, and it's one of Christianity's mega words. It means 'undeserved favour', or 'mercy', but you can popularise it by letting the five letters stand for **G**reat **R**iches **a**t **C**hrist's **E**xpense. St Paul put it this way, "For you know the *grace* of our Lord Jesus Christ, that though he was rich, yet for your sakes he became poor, so that you through his poverty might become rich." (St Paul's 2nd letter to the Corinthians, chapter 8, verse 9) Jesus abandoned the richness of divinity to assume the poverty of humanity, but having assumed it, then to transform it! As one early Christian leader put it, "Jesus became what we were that we might become what he is." Did we deserve this gracious act? Hardly, but then if we had been worthy of his love, it would not have been grace, and amazing grace at that!

By any reckoning, Jesus of Nazareth was extraordinary, a complete one-off. Even those who reject his claim to be divine nonetheless stand in awe of him. "I am not a believer," said H.G. Wells, "but this penniless preacher from Galilee is irresistibly the centre of history." A church hoping to attract enquirers to a study course on the Gospels placed this advertisement in their local paper: "Born in poverty, lived only thirty-three years. Spent much of his life in obscurity. Never wrote a book. Never had any position in public life. Was crucified with two thieves. And yet two thousand years later more than one billion people follow him. Surely it must be worthwhile to find out more about Jesus of Nazareth."

Christianity offers a radically new ethic, or code of conduct

In recent years the use of the letters BC (Before Christ) and AD (Anno Domini, the year of the Lord) to delineate the passage of time has died out in favour of BCE (Before the Common Era) and CE (Common Era). One reason given for the change was not to cause offence in our global village to the millions of non-Christians who could not acknowledge in any way the supremacy of Christ. A change engineered as a politically correct snub to Christians? Perhaps, but all is not lost: CE can be read as Christian Era, but more tellingly, subversively even, AD can stand for 'All Different'. Because that is exactly the case - post BC and in 'the years of our Lord', nothing remained the same, the world would be changed for ever!

How so? For the simple reason that "the grace of our Lord Jesus Christ" overflowed! Joyfully received by his followers, they passed it on - they had to, compelled by his love; and the effects were gradually felt throughout the whole Roman Empire. So copying Jesus' example, members of the fledgling Christian communities began to care for the poor, the sick and the outcasts of society. It was Christians who founded the first hospitals, and it was Christians who counter-culturally began to look after the many orphaned and abandoned children. When a plague killed up to five million people in the AD 170s, it was Christians who stayed in the afflicted urban areas to care for the dying.

Come nearer to our times, and discover the deeply committed Christian Member of Parliament, William Wilberforce, passion-ately fighting to end the slave trade; see Lord Shaftesbury, the 'reforming earl' as he was known, driven by his faith to plead the cause of boy chimney sweeps despite endless setbacks. In his book, 'The Cross and Crescent', Colin Chapman explains the rise, and growth down the AD centuries, of this revolutionary ethic: "The Incarnation will constantly call us to leave the safety of our own circle, and to reach out to that other community or individual in love and hope."

So what about the Crusades, the Spanish Inquisition, child sex abuse, and other Church-sponsored horrors?

Terrible. Jesus weeps. Enfeebled by a combination of greed, power-lust and misguided religious zeal - primeval human urges, all three - the Church, the institution that is, became corrupted by the very world of politics, education and commerce within which Jesus had intended his followers to be purifying salt and light. Secular movements aiming for change have universally fared no better. Communism, for example, despite its noble and in some ways Christian aspirations, quickly mutated to monster-mode, consigning millions to untold misery and oppression. It all boils down to the well-worn aphorism: "the corruption of the best leads always to the worst," but that doesn't thereby invalidate the best's contribution.

'All Different' infiltrated the world in other ways. It gave society a piece of new vocabulary, the word forgiveness, a concept almost unknown BCE outside Judaism. The Jews had adopted the maxim: "Love your neighbour and hate your enemies", but Jesus told his followers, "Love your enemies, and pray for those who persecute you" (St Matthew, chapter 5, verses 43-44); an ethical bombshell, that has filled the history books with countless examples of ordinary Christians who have forsaken the traditional paths of bitter reprisal and revenge, offering a better way that has sometimes brought their oppressors to their knees.

There is an African proverb which runs, "A Christian is someone who walks on two legs: grace and forgiveness." Nelson Mandela was one such African. This man entered prison as an angry insurrectionist, and emerged twenty-four years later as a convinced disciple of Jesus Christ. On becoming South Africa's president, he invited his former jailor, a white man, to attend the inauguration ceremony as a VIP guest; and the prosecutor at his trial came to lunch at his residence. When the widow of Hendrik Verwoerd, one of the architects of apartheid, was prevented by illness from attending a President's tea party for wives of members of the racist Nationalist Party, Mandela made a special point of visiting her. Amazing grace!

And in the UK, who can forget Gee Walker, a person of colour and mother of eighteen-year-old Anthony, who was killed in Liverpool in 2005 in a brutal racist attack? Outside the courtroom when her son's murderer was convicted and jailed, she said, "I have got to forgive him. Forgiveness is my survival tool. If we did not forgive, it would have destroyed us. Forgiveness frees me up - to love; it brings me peace."

Me, a sinner? Surely not!

T he book's strap line speaks of 'God's **Rescue Pack...**' But what if I feel no need of being rescued? If I'm fine as I am, what has Christianity to say to me?

I am writing this book in the spring and summer of 2020, when the whole world is in the grip of the Coronavirus pandemic. Covid-19 has proved so dangerous partly because you could have it without knowing it, what was termed 'asymptomatic'. Worse, in that condition, you could pass it on to large numbers of people, again without realising the harm involved. One of the Christian Faith's foundational tenets is that every single human being is infected with a potentially fatal spiritual virus passed on from one generation to the next; and you can be inflicted with it without knowing or acknowledging the fact! So we really do need a 'vaccine', an antidote, a rescue!

This sober appraisal is found in the Jewish Scriptures, and to an extent in classical Greek philosophy. In the 4th century BCE, Plato described the human being as a charioteer with two horses to drive. One horse is gentle, biddable and obedient to words of command. It is called 'Reason'. The other horse is wild, untamed and rebellious. It is called 'Passion'.

So which is in 'the driving seat'? When life is going smoothly, we can be polite, even charming, outward looking and caring, 'nice' people in fact. But put us under pressure, and that pleasant veneer is quickly stripped away. In her book 'Leningrad', Anna Reid describes the grotesque effects of starvation inflicted on the city's population during the siege of 1941-1944. "Sadder, perhaps, even than physical breakdown was the way in which hunger destroyed personalities and relationships." She quotes a resident's eyewitness testimony, "Before the war, people adorned themselves with bravery, fidelity to principles, and honesty. The hurricane of war has torn off those rags: now everyone has become *what he was in fact, and not what he wanted to seem.*" An Auschwitz survivor, put to work at the camp's crematoria, said, "Every person, *without exception*, is capable of doing the worst things, just to live another minute." (Italics mine)

Aren't those rather extreme examples, the exception not the norm?

Maybe, but they illustrate the fundamental human paradox, expressed by Blaise Pascal, the 17th century French scientist: "Man is neither an angel, nor a beast, and the sad thing is that the would-be angel becomes an actual beast."

Building on its Jewish foundations, Christianity's New Testament ruthlessly probes this innate beastliness, using the well-known 'S' word - sin! What is sin? Forgive the simple crudity, but take the word's three letters:

'S' stands for '**S**hove off, God.' The very first sin recorded in the Bible, the original sin if you like (!), was not one of the headline hitters - murder, rape, theft or perjury. It was simply a declaration of human independence from God, a rejection of his divine authority as the Creator. (Genesis, chapter 3, verses 1-7)

So the 'I' of 'sin' stands for 'I'm in charge', or 'I in the centre'. Isn't this exactly our nature? Just as my computer has certain default settings, I naturally default to an unattractive self-centredness that is potentially harmful to those around me.

The 'N' of 'sin' drives this home: it stands for 'No rules', or 'Not your rules, God'. "I will do things my way."

The Jewish Scriptures describe what happened when the human race did it their way. With God shown the door, things went downhill fast. The world sank into murderous violence, economic exploitation, racial strife, family disintegration and more, much more. The environment was adversely affected. Not so very different from the world's condition ever since, and still today. There is so much that's wrong in the world, but God isn't to blame, we are!

You say 'we', but most of the world's problems are caused by 'the system', the greedy multinationals, globalisation and all that.

The 'system' as you call it is certainly a breeding ground for manipulation and exploitation, but it is you and I, along with millions of others global-wide, who constitute and sustain it. Unwittingly perhaps, we are cogs in a vast machine, tiny cogs maybe, but nevertheless bearing a degree of responsibility. A professional economist, himself a Christian, put it like this: "You can be a lawyer, never overcharge your client, never fiddle your expenses, but through your agility with tax laws on behalf of a multinational mining organisation, be involved in the systematic impoverishment of the nation whose ore the company has extracted, but to whom no tax has been paid." So you and I may well be guilty – by association!

The Old Testament talks a lot about sin, but Jesus taught about love, so why should we be so bothered about sin?

Perhaps you need to take a closer look at what Jesus actually said! He was once asked whether eating food without first performing ritual ablutions spoilt a person's relationship with God, as some Jewish sects maintained. Did it make that person spiritually unclean? His reply was devastating. "It's not what goes into a person," he said, "that makes them unclean. It's what comes **out** of a person that defiles them." He continued by listing no less than thirteen possible evils gestating deep in the cesspit of the human heart: "evil thoughts, sexual immorality, theft, murder, adultery, greed, malice, deceit, lewdness, envy, slander, arrogance and folly." (St Mark, chapter 7, verses 20-23)

What a mouthful from this Jesus of love! And we can't help noticing something there. At least three of the sins listed are in the realm of thoughts or attitudes, not actions. Sin is not just what I do or say, Jesus said, it's about what I think as well.

So I defy anyone reading Jesus' words to deny that at least one of those thirteen is a correct diagnosis of what lies within them; within what Malcolm Muggeridge, 20th century sceptic and author later turned Christian, described as "the dark little dungeon of my own ego". This book's strapline is valid: we do need a rescue package!

But we need it not just because our existence on earth is seriously spoiled by a spiritual disease. We have a greater problem that reaches into eternity. Tune more deeply into Jesus' teaching once more, and we come across this sombre warning from his lips:

"If you do not believe that I am the one I claim to be, you will indeed die in your sins." (St John, chapter 8, verse 24) What did Jesus mean by this enigmatic phrase: "die in your sins"? He was referring to the plight of someone who dies with their sins not properly dealt with, their errors unconfessed, unforgiven by God, and therefore hanging round their neck like a crushing weight. To use another picture, they die with a lengthy indictment against their name, an enormous debt on their spiritual 'account'. What happens to someone who, standing alone, faces their Creator in such a state? There can only be one just answer: their Creator's righteous judgement, or punishment, eternal exclusion from his perfect Kingdom. A terrible prospect, but it doesn't have to happen. God doesn't want it to happen! Hence the mission of Jesus, his love-driven rescue pack, ours for the taking.

Earlier on in St John's Gospel, the author pens one of the most memorable statements in the whole of the Bible, a priceless summary of this Christian hope: "For God so *loved* the world that he gave his one and only Son, that whoever believes in him should not *perish* but have eternal life." (St John, chapter 3, verse 16 - italics mine)

What about all the good things we do? Don't they balance out the bad things?

The Christian Faith never denies our inherent ability to do good deeds, to perform acts of noble courage, even; and Christians are encouraged so to live; but the essence of sin, our defiantly and persistently 'putting two fingers up at God' can never be compensated by bursts of benevolence. For one thing, our motives for doing good are tainted by a measure of self-interest ("what will this do for me," we ask, "for my quest for self-fulfilment, and my reputation?"), and so often we fail to live consistently. As George Orwell put it: "On the whole, human beings want to be good, but not too good, and not quite all the time." (!) So my good deeds remind me of that snowfall last winter. How pristine white and pure those snowflakes looked! But when I melted a handful of snow in a cup, the water was grubby, and unfit to drink.

More fundamental, however, is the Bible's assertion that God's authority or law does not consist of hundreds of rules, some to be kept, some to be broken, but rather in a single perfect standard, call it 'his will'. Break this law at just one point, and it's broken in entirety, just as a single spot of grease on the bride's wedding dress ruins the whole outfit. I vividly recall the moment when I sent my very first e-mail, or tried to! I made one small mistake in the address, only one - a hyphen instead of an underscore - but that was sufficient for the entire post to be rejected!

What about all those who are ignorant of God's will, because they've never had the opportunity to hear it?

Jesus clearly taught that in the final reckoning, and he was adamant there will be one, God would take account of unavoidable ignorance. (St Luke, chapter 12, verses 47-48) However, the basic principle still stands: ignorance of the law is no excuse. I mentioned my first e-mail just now; my first attempt at ten-pin bowling was equally inglorious. I sent a scorcher down the alley achieving a strike, but the po-faced scoreboard registered '0'. I had committed a foot fault. "But I didn't know about foot faults, nobody told me," I angrily mouthed to the screen. No answer. Excuse rejected. Score: zero.

One of Jesus' most famous followers, St Paul, teaches in one of his letters that God has revealed some truth about himself, however little, to all humankind without exception: the witness of nature, for example, to his glory and power. No one therefore is without some degree of responsibility for the choices they make. (Romans, chapter 1, verse 18-20)

I know I have done wrong things, but it's not my fault; everything in life has been loaded against me.

That's sad to hear, but to be honest it reminds me of that time-honoured poster which read: "It's not your fault. It's the fault of the person standing next to you." The blame game - and we humans are masters at it! Some years ago, the head chef of a prestigious international airline cited base human nature as the reason for so many unjustified complaints from passengers about the in-flight food. "It's always the airline meal that's made them ill," he chided, "never the hamburger or curry they ate the night before, or the bottle of vodka they've consumed on the flight, or even the excitement of going away." We mentioned earlier the Bible story about the very first sin committed. When the Lord confronted the two perpetrators with their disobedience, they didn't own up. Instead, they blamed each other, then God, and then the Devil! Not a hint of an apology or admission of guilt! (Genesis, chapter 3, verses 11-13)

And passing the buck has been our over-defensive default position from time immemorial. We blame our genes, the government, grandparents, and global forces, anyone or anything apart from ourselves. No wonder the Christian Faith presents us all with a stern challenge: will we always assume the role of victim, but never the villain? Forever deprived, but never depraved? Emil Brunner, the famous 20th century Swiss theologian, put it this way: "Christianity is the only religion that strips us naked and declares us bankrupt in the sight of God."

This has been a very full justification of our need for 'rescue', but without the Christian Faith's 'bad news' we cannot appreciate its good news! Something Jesus' friend, Peter, once wrote sums this up: "Christ has given us his very great promises, so that through them you may...escape the *corruption* in the world caused by *evil* desires." (St Peter's 2nd letter, chapter 1, verses 3-4) (italics mine)

What is a Christian?

What is a Christian, and how has he or she been 'rescued'? You might suggest some popular answers like these:

A Christian is someone who helps others and believes in doing good.

That is an important part of being a Christian, certainly, but there are many atheists and agnostics who do a lot of good, so there must be something more to being a Christian.

A Christian is someone who believes in God.

Believing in God is an essential part of being a Christian, but Jews and Muslims believe strongly in God too, so there must be something more to being a Christian.

A Christian is someone who goes to church.

Going to church is an important part of being a Christian, but merely entering a purpose-built Christian building doesn't prove anything in itself, just as putting a wheelbarrow into a garage doesn't turn it into a car!

So what is a Christian then? Let's look at the actual word. How does it spell out?

CHRISTIAN

If we drop the 'A', we get

CHRIST IN

We're getting a bit nearer to the answer: a Christian is a 'Christ-in', or someone who is 'in Christ'. This Christ is of course Jesus, the Jesus Christ of the Bible, and a Christian is someone who has in some way built a relationship with him. There has been a coming together, or bond of unity formed, with Jesus.

Wasn't Jesus Christ dead and buried two thousand years ago? So how can I possibly have a relationship with him, or be 'in him', as you say?

A fair question, but you are only half right. Jesus was definitely dead and buried, but that wasn't the end of the story! He was crucified on a Friday, but on the very next Sunday God raised him from death, and enabled him to appear very much alive to many of his friends. Now this may sound far-fetched – it has never happened to anyone before or since - but there is circumstantial evidence for Jesus' resurrection, both in the Bible and in other historical documents. The evidence is overwhelming! (More on this later.)

Try picking up a Bible and reading the story for yourself. It's found in the last chapters of what we referenced earlier: 'The

Gospels', or 'Good News Stories', four of them: Matthew, Mark, Luke and John.

So if Jesus rose again from death, it follows that in some way, he is still alive; and if he's still alive, it is possible that he can be a real, living presence – **'in'** people, and they **'in'** him.

This relationship with Jesus we're talking about – what difference does it make to someone's life? How would being in this relationship change my life?

Another good question, and the answer lies in several great statements Jesus once made about himself, some of them claims that no other rational human being in history has ever dared to make. They are so off the wall that they must be either completely bogus, or backed up as true by his unique victory over death.

Let's look at the first of these statements, in fact the very first public words Jesus spoke as he began to teach and preach in about AD30 in the land we now call Israel, or Palestine.

Jesus' claims

Jesus said, *"The Kingdom of God is near. Repent and believe the good news."* (St Mark, chapter 1, verse 15)

By 'the Kingdom of God', Jesus means any place, time or sphere of human existence where God in some way or another is exercising authority as the Ruler. In practice? Where his name is being honoured and not misused as a swear word! Where his values, such as the Ten Commandments, are followed. Where his justice, righteousness and love are moulding individuals, communities, and even nations, towards the welfare of all. Jesus is claiming that his arrival has brought this long-awaited global improvement a whole lot closer! By his inspirational example, healings and teaching, Jesus demonstrates how different life can be when men and women submit to God's laws and values.

Subsequently Jesus went on to recruit his first disciples, the first 'Christians' you could say. He called them to follow his example by remodelling their lives according to the Kingdom's values, and thereby attract others to make God their Ruler.

So a Christian is someone beginning to recognise the Kingdom of God. Aware of their need to bring God, or Jesus, the true

King, more into their lives, they have begun to de- throne 'self' as the Number One. This is not easy! It requires a step-change Jesus called 'repentance,' but he also proclaimed 'good news', good news to be believed about him and what he can do for those who put themselves 'in-him'.

What is this 'good news', or gospel? The answer lies in more of those claims of Jesus. Seven of them, all charged with great significance, are recorded in the fourth Gospel, the Gospel of John. Why seven? One for each day of the week?! Maybe, but it's really more subtle than that. In the Bible, the number seven never stands only for the literal one above six, and one below eight. Instead seven stands for 'completeness', or the very essence of something; just as when we talk of a mariner 'sailing the seven seas', we don't mean seven different areas of water, we mean the entire surface of the oceans planet- wide. So in making his seven great statements, each about his identity and beginning with the words "I am", Jesus is laying claim to a cosmic fullness, nothing less than the essence of God himself. Let's look at them in turn.

"I am the Bread of Life. The one who comes to me will never go hungry." (St John, chapter 6, verse 35)

We all need physical food, but Jesus offers a different sort of food, nourishment for our spiritual life, or our 'soul', to use an old-fashioned term. Life as we experience it invites us to feed on many philosophies, ideologies and escapist routes (such as self-fulfilment, fame, wealth and bodily prowess) to satisfy our appetite for meaning and purpose, but they all leave us 'hungry' in the end, dissatisfied and empty. Not so Jesus and his truth, his bread!

Three years after becoming a Christian, a young adult from a nominally religious background, wrote this: "For over three years now, Jesus Christ has filled my life in a way that I could never have achieved. He has made complete and whole the puzzle that was me. He has filled the voids with himself and his love."

Key word: COME A Christian is someone who, like a beggar asking for bread, has come to Jesus with empty hands outstretched to receive what he has to offer.

Key truth: Jesus can rescue us from filling our lives with spiritual 'junk food.'

For further thought: the significance of Holy Communion

On the last night of his life, the night that he was betrayed to his enemies, Jesus shared a special meal with his friends. On the menu was bread. Towards the end of the meal, Jesus did an extraordinary thing. He took a chunk of the bread, broke it in two, and passed it round the table, for each guest to share a piece. As the bread was being passed round, Jesus said, "This is my body given for you; do this in remembrance of me." (St Luke, chapter 22, verse 19)

At the time, Jesus' friends did not understand his meaning, but after his death and resurrection, it struck them like a thunderbolt! The broken bread they had eaten that fateful night was a sign of Jesus' body, to be fearfully broken the very next day on a Roman cross. Yes, Jesus was indeed 'the Bread of Life' as he had claimed earlier, but he, the Bread, could not fully meet the spiritual needs of hungry men and women without being broken, offered in sacrifice, a sacrifice for sins. And his friends would not be able to benefit from that sacrifice without their 'sharing' in the bread, without receiving Jesus internally by faith, deep within spiritually, as deeply as when they ate some food.

The author celebrating Holy Communion on the shores of the Sea of Galilee

"Do this in remembrance of me," he had said, thereby inaugurating the most well-known of the future Christian Church's services, Holy Communion, or the Catholic Mass. Down the centuries, Christians have debated vigorously - far too vigorously at times! - what exactly happens to the bread when it is taken and blessed, or consecrated, by a religious officiant, or priest. Does it remain simply a concoction of flour and water, and so only a token memorial of Jesus' body, albeit a powerful symbol; or does it change in some mystical way into the actual body of Christ?

Some Christians have found it helpful to think of the bread (technically called 'the sacrament') as being like a wedding ring or engagement ring. At one level, a ring is only a circular piece of metal, even if materially precious like gold; and in the same way the bread of Holy Communion can be no more than a portion of ordinary bread. The wedding ring, however, gains enormous significance because of the momentous **words** of commitment uttered – "with this ring, I thee wed…" – and the powerful sacramental **act** of being offered and received onto the finger of the willing hand outstretched. Thereby imbued with such significance, the ring becomes hugely valued, and is never treated casually by the wearer. Just so with the bread of Holy Communion: the **words** spoken ("The Body of Christ which is given for you", or similar), together with the symbolic **act** of internal consumption, endow the purely physical with immense spiritual authority. No Christian ever receives communion lackadaisically – at least, they shouldn't!

It's no coincidence that of all possible foodstuffs, Jesus chose the humble loaf as his emblem, the poor man's staple fare. It sends a powerful message: all are precious to God, irrespective of rank or wealth; and even the simplest and most lowly of people can find true worth as his followers and in his service.

"I am the Light of the World. Whoever follows me will never walk in darkness, but will have the light of life." (St John,

chapter 8, verse 12)

We all need guidance in treading life's perplexing path into an unknown future. In her book 'Harry and the Philosopher's Stone', J K Rowling puts these significant words on the lips of Dumbledore, the Principal of Hogwart's Hall: "The trouble is, humans do have a knack of choosing precisely those things which are worst for them." He was right, but through his teaching and example, and by his living presence in relationship with us, Jesus can help us steer in the right direction, God's way. This will save and protect us from the dark consequences of unwise decisions and harmful behaviour, enabling us to reflect more of his light and love to others.

Having ignored God for most of his long life, a pensioner I knew who turned to Christ after attending church for a few months, described what had happened to him like this: "Becoming a Christian is like driving out of fog at night into a well-lit street area, and recognising where you are. It gives you a new set of priorities, because you want to go 'higher and higher', and you can never be complacent."

Key word: Follow A Christian is someone who FOLLOWS Jesus and so is called a disciple, another word for apprentice.

Key truth: Jesus can rescue us from wandering through life's maze without any moral compass, uncertain of the right path to follow, or values to adopt.

So which way now, then?

It would be wrong to conclude this paragraph without a warning! Following Jesus will not be a bed of roses! He described it as 'taking up the cross', in other words a life, like his, of self-sacrifice and possible suffering on his behalf. "If they persecuted me," he said, "they will persecute you too." (St John, chapter 15, verse 20)

For further thought: what does it mean to be 'born again'?

In common with other world religions, Christianity touches frequently on the themes of light and darkness, but instead of teaching a philosophical way of enlightenment, as in Buddhism, the Christian Faith speaks more of a crucial journey we need to take, a vital transfer, from one sphere of influence, the Kingdom of darkness or evil, to its nemesis, the Kingdom of Light or righteousness.

Addressing some pagans recently turned Christian, St Paul writes of "God the Father who has qualified you to share in the Kingdom of Light, for he has rescued us from the dominion of darkness and brought us into the Kingdom of the Son he loves." (Paul's letter to the Colossians, chapter 1, verses 12- 13) A baby's birth can provide a picture. From the moment of conception, a human foetus is alive, in one sense, feeding and moving; but it resides in the dark, its mother's womb. To be truly alive, the baby must travel out of the uterus through the woman's vagina into the world of light; it has to be born! In the same way, for a human being to experience the light of God's Kingdom, he or she has to be born - spiritually, 'born' a second time, however old physically, and so transferred away from their erstwhile habitat, the 'womb' of darkness. In practice this rebirth occurs when someone turns away from their sins and turns to Christ for forgiveness and the gift of his Spirit. Rebirth of this kind need not be a sudden, dramatic, 'Damascus-road' process; more often than not, being 'born again', or 'regeneration' as Christian vocabulary sometimes terms it, is a gradual progression, a spiritual journey, although often kick- started by some seminal moment of commitment.

I always thought 'born again' referred to happy-clappy, Bible punching believers?

Sadly the phrase has been hijacked to describe a certain type of Christian, but the resulting tag 'born again Christian' is tauto-logical nonsense. There are not two categories of Christian, the born again and the rest. The Bible is clear: if you have become a Christian by turning to Christ, his Spirit has entered into you, causing you to be born again whether or not you can articulate that. You have received a new life! You have travelled to the edge of a new world. St Paul put it like this: "If anyone is **IN** Christ, they are a new creation, the old has gone, the new has come." (St Paul's 2ⁿᵈ letter to the Corinthians, chapter 5, verse 17) The world famous American preacher, Dr Billy Graham, used to say this, "A Christian is not someone who tries again, rather someone who has been born again; not someone who has turned over a new leaf, but who has received a new life."

It's vital to grasp that it's not only obvious sinners and the downright irreligious that need this new birth. Jesus once spoke to a man called Nicodemus. This leader amongst the Jews was a respectable, upright citizen, a Pharisee who practised his religion scrupulously; but even to him, Jesus said, "You must be born again. No one can see the Kingdom of God unless they are born again of the Spirit." (St John, chapter 3, verses 3,5,7) To be religious doesn't get you there, Nicodemus! It's relationship that matters, a relationship with me, the Light of the World.

This anonymous confession from a university lecturer says it all: "I'm nice to my students, respectful to my colleagues, love my family, do not steal, commit adultery, use drugs or swear. But when I look at myself honestly, I see that I harbour bitterness, hoard my time and resent others intruding on me. I'm vain, and consumed with how others perceive me. I pretend to listen, but do not. I think more about being great than being good. My only hope is God."

"I am the Gate for the sheep; whoever enters through me will be saved." (St John, chapter 10, verses 7,9)

Jesus' claim to be 'the gate for the sheep', or 'door' as in some versions, sounds strange to our 21st century ears, but he is drawing substantially on traditional Jewish ideas: God's children, his 'flock', could not be allowed to wander through a dangerous and unrighteous world unprotected. Many hostile forces, including idolatrous paganism and the seductive lure of the occult, would be conspiring to turn them away from the one and only God, drawing them into evil ways. So like vulnerable sheep, they needed a fold to provide security, especially in the hours of 'darkness' when perils lurked and predators prowled. In short, a 'place' of refuge close to God himself was essential, a 'place' to be 'saved', or 'safe' to use Jesus' word.

The spiritual 'sheep pen' thus provided would be built with sturdy walls to deter would-be intruders, but also with a single gate for entry, a gate that could be closed to the undesirable, and opened only for the sheep. The Jewish Scriptures - what Christians call the 'Old Testament' - abounded in promises that God would one day send a uniquely perfect prophet-king, a Messiah-like figure, to act as the all important portal. Jesus' staggering claim here is that he was the fulfilment of all those ancient promises! He would be that gate, or sole entry point. To paraphrase slightly, he alone would be the gate keeper, enabling intimate access to the safety of God's love and protection.

The Christian Faith, as subsequently taught by Jesus and his disciples, builds on this very Jewish construct. Evil forces hover nearby just as much today as they did in Jesus' time, "sinful desires which war against the soul", to quote Peter, one of Jesus' friends. From these invisible but powerful enemies, we need to 'be saved', a safe 'place', a fold, the protection of God. But how to find such intimacy with God? Through Jesus, the one and only way or door, through which everyone, Jew or Gentile, must pass in order to know God.

(We shall return to this exclusive claim of Christianity when we look at the sixth of St John's "I am" sayings.)

Key truth: a Christian is someone who, realising the danger of walking through life spiritually alone and unprotected from evil, has sought their Creator's guardian presence through the one he has sent, Jesus Christ.

Key word: ENTER. The word suggests some kind of 'movement,' or step of faith towards Jesus.

For further thought: what does the Bible say about authentic leadership?

At the same time as making his claim to be 'the Gate', and therefore the entry point to safety, Jesus speaks of "thieves and robbers" (St John, chapter 10, verse 1), rustlers who will attempt to harm or steal the sheep, avoiding him, the door, by climbing over the wall at the far end of the fold. This is a warning about false leaders. They will try to infiltrate communities, religious or otherwise, to entice many to follow them, often with disastrous consequences.

Jesus had two contemporary scenarios in mind, one political, one religious. He was keenly aware that politically, his part of the world was in turmoil. Again and again hot-headed Jewish nationalists, the so-called zealots, had issued a call to arms against the Roman occupation forces, a futile cause doomed to failure. All such uprisings - and there would be more, equally unsuccessful, in the next few decades - had been brutally suppressed with considerable bloodshed: God's 'flock' had been ripped apart, literally. If only they would stay 'in the fold', reject false leaders, and follow his leadership that offered a far safer way, God's way, the way of peace.

Although uttered two thousand years ago, this warning from Jesus still speaks loudly today: whom do we choose as our political leaders? Hot-headed firebrands speciously promising some golden age? Nationalist zealots? Or men and women of integrity, wisdom and a temperate spirit? Trustworthy 'shepherds', to anticipate Jesus' next great claim.

Religious leadership was Jesus' second focus. Just before claiming to be the gate, he had clashed with a group called the Pharisees. In their role as the 'clergy' of the day, they were supposed to be the nation's spiritual guardians or shepherds. Tragically, however, they had repeatedly shown themselves to be arrogant, self-righteous, money grabbing, and deeply hostile to Jesus' penetrating and thoroughly justified rebukes. So they had proved to be the very antithesis of godly leadership, and in consequence a real threat to the spiritual wellbeing of the flock. Here and on other occasions, Jesus warns the common people against them in the strongest possible terms - they are just some of those "thieves and robbers" gate-crashing the fold for their own ends!

In some respects, not a lot has changed. It doesn't take much historical research to unearth the dismal fact that over the centuries, religions and their institutions, the Christian Church included, have proved a fertile hunting ground for the avaricious and power-hungry. A recent example would be a bishop in a developing country, who became a henchman of his country's new leader, strong-arming his flock to toe the nefarious presidential party line. Through other "thieves and robbers" like him, far too many 'sheep' have been conned, robbed, neglected, malnourished, bullied and exploited.

All of which inclines me to write off the Christian Church altogether, and even the Christian Faith it claims to represent.

That would be an unfortunate overreaction. Every institution, however noble its pedigree, has harboured its "wolf in sheep's clothing" from time to time. Let's not throw the baby out with the bath water, just because of a few high profile rotten apples in the ecclesiastical barrel!

The Christian Faith, through its handbook, the Bible, has a lot to say about leadership, good and bad, and not just in the arena of church or religion. Leaders in industry, commerce, education, the law, politics, even sport and the arts, could learn so much from reading the Book of Proverbs, for example.

So what we should we look for in our church leaders? The very opposite of thieves and robbers: givers, not grabbers. Strong shepherds, Jesus-like.

To interrupt the flow a moment, we can't help noticing that

Jesus introduces each of his seven claims with the simplest of expressions: "I am." To our ears, the present tense first person singular of the verb 'to be' is unremarkable, but to the listening Jews, hearing the words in their Hebrew equivalent, "I am" would have raised the hairs on the back of their neck. For "I am" in Hebrew was none other than the name, the awesome and almost unmentionable name, of the Lord himself, Jehovah, Yahweh, the God who centuries before had appeared to Moses, revealing himself to be "I am who I am." (Exodus, chapter 3, verse 14) So by front-loading each of his momentous claims with "I am", Jesus was at the very least hinting at his divine status, if not actually stating it.

So what about the title 'Son of God' often accredited to Jesus? Does this mean he was 50% human and 50% divine, or some kind of spiritual hybrid?

Christians have wrestled to square that particular circle from the very beginning; in fact in the first few centuries, they argued furiously with each other about the exact nature of Jesus, and whether he had two natures or one! The simplest fall-back position is to say that Jesus was 100% God and 100% human, such that he presented not an artificial humanity nor a diluted divinity. You could maintain that his humanity was as beautifully perfect, or divine, as God had originally created every human to be.

The title 'Son of God' does not mean that Jesus enjoyed a lower status of divinity, or minor royal mode; neither does it mean that God the Father had a wife, as, sadly, scoffers mockingly suggest. No, 'son of...' is an intensely Semitic expression, meaning the 'exact expression of', the 'splitting image of'. So after living cheek by jowl with his friends for three years, Jesus can say to those who must have known him through and through, "Anyone who has seen me has seen the Father." (St John, chapter 14, verse 9) It is, of course, yet another of Jesus' stupendous claims; and it makes the next of his "I am…" sayings even more remarkable.

"I am the Good Shepherd. The Good Shepherd lays down his life for the Sheep." (St John, chapter 10, verse 11)

Here Jesus is predicting his future death. It will take place in Jerusalem on the day we call Good Friday. He will be no stranger to intense, undeserved suffering, which in itself may attract us to him. The mystery of unjust suffering lies right at the heart of Christianity.

Every good shepherd cares for their flock, and loves them whatever the cost. In the same way, it was Jesus' love for all humankind, prone to going astray like sheep, that drove him to sacrifice himself.

But what did his sacrifice achieve for you and me? One verse from the Bible puts it this way: "Christ died **for** our sins." (1st Corinthians, chapter 15, verse 3) **For:** that is, because of our sins, or owing to them. It was human wickedness, in which we all share to some degree, that put him, the totally innocent, on the cross. However, Jesus also died **for** our sins in order to deal with them, by paying the price they deserved. By his death on the cross, Jesus has carried away our sins, neutralising or detoxifying them. This frees those who trust in Jesus from guilt,

43

shame and the fear of future divine judgement.

Key word: TRUST Just as sheep TRUST their shepherd to deliver them from predators, a Christian is someone who has wholeheartedly trusted in Jesus to free them, through his death, from the grip of sin and evil.

Key truth: Jesus can rescue us from trying to hide our faults, or making excuses; and he can save us from eternal exclusion from God's Kingdom.

(Obviously these third and fourth claims overlap somewhat. Can Jesus be both the gate, and the shepherd? Actually, yes! At nightfall, a Palestinian shepherd in Jesus' time would himself lie down across the entrance to the fold. A dual role, gate and guardian. Any would-be predator would have to climb over his recumbent body, if they dared!)

For further thought: a closer look at the Easter story

Biographies of famous people do not usually concentrate on their celebrity's death. More often than not, their passing is recorded briefly, almost as a postscript, not a major theme. Not so with Jesus of Nazareth. Between them, the four Gospels add up to eighty-nine chapters. Of these twenty-nine, or thirty-two percent, are about the last week in Jesus' life, culminating in his death and resurrection.

The story is bloody, a far cry from Easter bunnies and chocolate. First, Jesus was blindfolded and beaten up; then brutally flogged, before being put to death by crucifixion, probably the cruellest and most protracted method of execution ever invented. However the Bible accounts do not dwell on the physical pain, partly because public crucifixions were commonplace in the Roman world, so making a gore fest of the story was unnecessary. More to the point was the tsunami of human evil that drove the events of that infamous day.

On the 25 May 2020, a black American citizen, George Floyd, was killed by a white policeman in Minneapolis. An outraged nation erupted into public protests with many white people joining in. Covering the story for the British Broadcasting Corporation, a journalist commented, "The murder of George Floyd has held up a mirror to the American people, and they do not like what they see." In the same way, the story of Jesus' Passion holds up a mirror - to the entire human race, and what do we see?

Firstly, the greed of Judas Iscariot, the disciple of Jesus who betrayed him to the authorities for a large sum of money; secondly, the envy of the Jewish religious authorities, insanely jealous of Jesus' popularity with the common people; thirdly, the cowardice of Pontius Pilate, the Roman Governor, who fearing for his job if he released Jesus, sentenced him to death whilst convinced of his innocence; fourthly the hysteria of the crowds swiftly whipped up into lynch-mode; finally, the coarse brutality and callous devotion to duty of the soldiers involved.

A grotesque potpourri of avarice, malice, fear, mania and sadism. Do we not see ourselves somewhere in this mirror? The Oberammergau Passion Play, performed every ten years, opens with this sombre statement: "Let each of us recognise his own guilt in these events." The nineteenth century Scottish hymn writer, Horatius Bonar, penned these memorable lines:

" 'Twas I that shed the sacred blood; I nailed him to the tree;
   I crucified the Christ of God; I joined the mockery."

This sobering perspective is hugely important if we are to appreciate the "Good Shepherd laying down his life for the sheep." Before we can begin to see the cross as something done **for** us, leading to faith and worship, we have to see it as something done **by** us, leading us to repentance.

The charred cross in the ruins of the old Coventry Cathedral

So what exactly was Jesus doing **for** us? He was dealing with our innate human wickedness, absorbing it, carrying it away, paying for it. No human illustration can fully plumb the depths, the mystery of the cross, but some stories may shed a ray of light:

On 15 March 2015, a suicide bomber entered a Christian church in Lahore, Pakistan. Two worshippers, a husband and wife, spotted the terrorist and, suspecting his intent, ran towards him, to embrace him, thus smothering the force of the blast. They perished, but saved many lives. By willingly going to his death on the cross, Jesus 'ran to embrace our sin', so muzzling its explosive power.

What power? The power, as explained earlier, to cut us off eternally from our holy and righteous Creator God. Grievous wrong towards God had been, and would be, committed by us. Estrangement the inevitable consequence. The only remedy? Reconciliation, and that is precisely the precious word the New Testament uses to describe what Jesus achieved by his voluntary sacrifice.

One of the most poignant verses in the entire New Testament puts it this way: "God was reconciling the world to himself in Christ, not counting people's sins against them." (St Paul's 2nd letter to the Corinthians, chapter 5, verse 19) Remove the cause of grievance, our sins, and reconciliation could occur; but if God were to delete our sins from the debit column of our spiritual bank account, so to speak, not counting them against us, what would he do with them? Forget them? Write them off? No, for to do either of those would leave heinous wrongdoing unrequited, unresolved. Not much justice or morality there! So what did God do with our sins? He transferred them to Jesus' account, Jesus the perfect one, the one and only living being with no sins to his name. See what St Paul goes on to say in verse 21: "God made him who had no sin to be sin for us."

This extraordinary divine move has been called 'the great exchange.' The famous German theologian, Martin Luther, put it this way: "Jesus - the greatest murderer, adulterer, swindler, and thief that the world has ever known, not because he committed those sins, but because he took them on behalf of those who did."

This exchange, or swop, happens to be providentially and brilliantly illustrated at the very heart of the Good Friday story. In the dock and facing a possible capital sentence with Jesus that morning was a murderer called Barabbas. The Roman governor, Pilate, was accustomed to releasing a convicted prisoner occasionally as a conciliatory gesture. So would it be Barabbas or Jesus? The innocent Jesus, surely! Justice demanded it, but no, Pilate, under pressure, selected Jesus to die, Barabbas to live. So the innocent and the guilty swopped places. Pilate's unworthy exchange led to Barabbas' great escape. It's a parable or picture: God's great exchange leads to our great escape.

Escape? Yes. Because our sins have been dealt with, God can forgive them, and so comprehensive is his forgiveness that the New Testament uses a whole cluster of different expressions to describe it: sins obliterated, washed away, covered over, cancelled, just some of the images used. William Barclay, the great Scottish author and theologian, sums up: "There is no book which has so great a sense of the horror of sin as the New

Testament, but equally there is no book which is so sure that the cure and the remedy have been found." So a local church was right on the mark when its outside notice board announced, "Trespassers will be forgiven." (!)

So God punishes Jesus, an innocent third party, for someone else's crimes. That sounds thoroughly immoral to me!

You have put your finger on one of the most frequent objections to the Easter message, as commonly misunderstood. Jesus was **not** a third party! Hard as this is to grasp, it's vital we try. Let's look again at exactly what St Paul said: "God was **in Christ** reconciling the world to himself." So God the Father and Christ the Son were in it together, right up to their necks. The God who "does not count people's sins against them" is the same God who then has those sins counted against him. God the Law Maker becomes in Jesus God the Law Breaker. Can you recall our description of the Godhead as a trinitarian community, three in one, and one in three, essentially united in a bond of love? Well, at Easter that divine community of love agreed to be torn apart, rent asunder, as the only way of satisfying justice and saving the sinner.

Nothing less than this can explain Jesus' agonising cry of dereliction as he hung on the cross: "My God, my God, why have you forsaken me?" (St Mark, chapter 15, verse 34) So at the very heart of the Christian story is suffering, the suffering of God.

What should our reaction be to all this? We wonder how Barabbas reacted! With astonishment? With incredulity? With a shrug of the shoulders? Or with shame mingled with deep gratitude, perhaps even leading him in the weeks that followed to become a Christian disciple? Down the centuries, people have responded to the cross in all of those different ways, and we, too, are free to choose. The story is told of a German student who visited an art gallery in the city of Dusseldorf. As he gazed at a painting of Jesus' crucifixion, he noticed an inscription below: "All this I have done for thee. What hast thou done for me?"

We notice the order of 'doing' in that inscription. It is God who has done something first, he has taken the initiative. So the cross of Christ does not present us immediately with a demand, rather an offer. Not "do this", but "this has been done" - for you, so receive it freely. We are not called to 'try a bit harder' but to take Christ's free gift of forgiveness. Then, and only then, comes our 'doing' bit: the commitment of our lives to Christ in gratitude for his undying love for us. As someone has said, "Christianity is not just a simple matter of 'give and take'; it's 'take, then give'".

"I am the Resurrection and the Life. The one who lives and believes in me will never die." (St John, chapter 11, verse 25)

Here Jesus predicts his own ultimate victory over death, which will take place in Jerusalem on the day we call Easter Sunday. But what does his resurrection mean for you and me? It means that our physical death need not signal the very end of us! There is new life on the other side of the grave; and if we are in-Christ, he carries us through death 'on his shoulders', so to speak.

This claim of Jesus is hugely important. It answers the age- old question that has troubled humankind from the very beginning: is there anything after death, and if so, what?

Key words: LIVE and BELIEVE. A Christian is someone who BELIEVES that Jesus was raised from the dead and LIVES a life of trust in him as their risen Lord and Master.

Key truth: Jesus can rescue us from loss of future hope, bitterness and cynicism, and the fear of death.

For further thought: the evidence for Jesus' resurrection

So Jesus would indeed "lay down his life for the sheep", but that would not be the end of the Good Shepherd! He would live again. There would be resurrection, predicted here by Jesus in this momentous claim. All four Gospels tell the same basic story. Executed by the Romans on the Friday, and duly certified as dead (St Mark, chapter 15, verses 42-45), Jesus' body was taken down from the cross by sympathisers, and laid in a hitherto unused tomb in a nearby garden. Some of Jesus' women disciples followed the sad procession, planning to return to mourn when the impending Sabbath, or Jewish Day of Rest, was over. They duly arrived back at the tomb very early on the Sunday morning, to discover to their horror that the large stone sealing the entrance had been rolled away, and Jesus' body removed. As they pondered what had happened, angelic messengers told them: "Jesus who was crucified, he has risen! He is not here." (St Mark, chapter 16, verse 6) So who moved the stone? Human beings, or ?

A 1st century AD rolling stone tomb, such as the one Jesus was laid in

The terrified and bewildered women raced away to pour it all out to the men disciples, who, true to form perhaps, at first dismissed their tale as nonsense. There is a refreshing frankness about these accounts of the men, the likes of Peter and John. They would shortly become the leaders of the fledgling Christian movement, but there is no attempt to spare their blushes!

The Gospels' narratives compel us to take the Easter Sunday story seriously in two other significant ways. Firstly, there is no eyewitness description of the actual moment the resurrected Jesus left his tomb, so we are spared the over- egged hype of a Hollywood blockbuster. Secondly, all four accounts agree that the first witnesses to the empty tomb, and to hear the angelic summons to spread the news, were women. This is extraordinary, given that in those days, a woman's testimony was not recognised in a court of law. No author, seeking to write up the resurrection story as a largely fictional piece of Christian propaganda, would have penned it in such daring terms!

The sceptic trying to rubbish the resurrection story must provide satisfactory answers to several awkward questions. To begin with, why was Jesus' tomb found empty when a mere thirty-six hours after his death, some of his women followers came back to the grave, knowing its exact location, to embalm his body? Perhaps Jesus' enemies had removed the body over the weekend, but if so, why did they not produce it as soon as resurrection rumours began to circulate, so at a stroke nipping the story in the bud? If Jesus' disciples stole the body, how come that one or more did not later spill the beans under torture by the hostile authorities? Men and women will gladly die for what they sincerely believe to be the truth, but not for what they know to be a lie.

Other questions present themselves: almost overnight, Jesus' friends morphed from being a frightened and disillusioned band of fugitives from the law, into an emboldened group fearlessly proclaiming in public that their former Master was Lord of all! Something very extraordinary must have occurred to bring about such change! Equally surprising was their swiftly adopted practice of 'breaking bread' in memory of Jesus' death, the service initially called 'The Lord's Supper', and later Holy Communion. If Jesus' crucifixion had been his ghastly end, why relive such a dismal and gruesome conclusion to the story? But if the crucified one had risen.....?

In addition, the resurrection is the only logical explanation for another change. These early Christians, Jews to the core, changed their day of worship from the seventh day of the week, the Saturday, the sacrosanct Jewish Sabbath, to the first day of the week, Sunday as we call it. Why? Unless something seismic had occurred on that day, something like a divine hand opening a sealed and strongly guarded tomb. (St Matthew, chapter 27, verses 62-66)

All of this can be researched in much more detail from websites such as www.bethinking.org.

So sceptics can be challenged, but Christians must also face some tricky questions.

Even if Jesus' resurrection is a historical fact, how can a miracle two thousand years ago, however unique, affect my death now? The answer is that Jesus' resurrection was not just an ancient story that Christians believe, it is an ongoing cosmic-wide event in which we can share! The Bible tells us that when we, by repentance and faith, commit ourselves to Christ, we move to a position of being '**in him**', that is inseparably linked to him, fused with him. So just as death could not hold him, could not prevent him emerging from the tomb into a radically new mode of existence, neither can a Christian's death hold him or her; rather it becomes the gateway to a whole new world, one day to be incorporated into God's promised new creation.

Think of it this way: in the days before the Anglo-French Channel Tunnel, there was only one way a motor car could access the European mainland - by being immersed deep within the bowels of an ocean going car ferry. Only such a unique, purpose-built vessel could transport the car safely through the watery depths. In the same way, only Christ, death's conqueror, can carry the frail and guilty sinner (and that's all of us, as we've said) through the waters of judgement that bar the way to eternal life. Christ is our 'car ferry', or ark as in the story of Noah, and the Christian is by repentance and faith immersed deep '**in him**'. Hence the claim of Jesus we're thinking about: "*I am the Resurrection and the Life. Whoever lives and believes **in** me will live, even though he dies.*" (St John 11: 25) St Paul wrote to a church in Asia Minor, "*Your life is now hidden with Christ **in** God*" (Colossians 3: 3).

For the Christian, having such a promised hope, will not necessarily diminish the trauma of the journey towards death, but it can give a profound sense of peace, and certainly a deep-rooted assurance that our eternal destiny is secure. Whilst serving as a parish priest, I visited in hospital a member of my congregation who had just been told that he was suffering from incurable cancer. Looking up at me from his bed, he said with a smile, "In a way this is a good thing, because I am so looking forward to seeing Jesus. He has become more wonderful the longer I have known him."

"*I am the Way, the Truth, and the Life. No one comes to the Father except through me.*" (St John, chapter 14, verse 6)

Many people believe in the existence of God, our Maker and the Creator of the universe. But how can we reach this God, and know him?

Jesus gives us a deeply thought-provoking answer. He, and he alone, is the Way **to** God, the Truth **about** God, and the Life **of** God. He therefore is the "narrow gate", through which we must enter to gain access to God. So what about Islam's Mohammed, or the Buddha, or Sikhism's Guru Nanak? Great teachers and inspirational leaders they may have been, but none of them led a perfect life, died a sacrificial death, or rose from the dead. Jesus did all three! He was, and is, unique, and he is therefore uniquely qualified to lead us to God.

Key word: COME A Christian is someone who, whilst respecting other world faiths, has humbly but firmly set their claims aside, and COME to Jesus exclusively.

Key truth: Jesus can rescue us from a bewildering choice of conflicting world views, and a doomed-to-fail quest for a life of perfection. Jesus anchors our lives on the firm foundation of his peerless life and teaching, his death and resurrection.

For further thought: why does Christianity make such exclusive claims?

Of all the "I am" claims of Jesus, this one from St John, chapter 14, verse 6 has drawn the most flak from many different quarters, religious, philosophical and social. "How outrageously narrow and exclusive!" cry the critics. "How dare Jesus claim that his is the only right path up the mountain." Perhaps it depends on the name or the 'height' of the mountain. Jesus, I suggest, is not negating all spiritual experience outside the Christian way. So the Muslim can certainly sense the power and protection of Allah, if Allah the inscrutable chooses to be merciful; but there is a higher peak: the privilege of knowing God intimately as our heavenly Father. Only one of the family, the Father's Son, can make the necessary introduction. Hence Jesus' carefully crafted claim: "No one comes **to the Father** except through me."

During the American Civil War, a soldier who had suffered a family tragedy and so wanted exemption from military service was told he could seek a hearing from the President. However, on arrival at the White House, he was refused entry. Sitting, disconsolate, in a nearby park, he was approached by a young boy to whom he poured out his story. Eventually the boy said, "Come with me." He then led the soldier back to the White House, and to the man's astonishment, was able to walk as far as the Oval Office without being challenged. Abraham Lincoln, standing there, turned and said, "What can I do for you, son?" The lad replied, "Dad, this soldier needs to talk to you." You want to reach the boss-man? Only through the son!

We may instinctively react against exclusivity in any sphere, but in fact we work with acceptable 'narrowness' every day. I have a bunch of Yale keys, and to me they look identical, but only one, just one, opens my front door, and that's the one I must select every time. I may not like that, but it's a fact! Or think of it like this: suppose a long-lost friend contacts you, suggesting you meet up. You both live some distance apart in rural areas, so you agree upon a certain large town as the rendezvous point. But where exactly in that town? How narrowly will you specify the location? As narrowly as possible, surely, to ensure you don't miss each other in a big place. So if Christianity seems to be narrow, it's not that God is playing hard to get, rather that he wants to be sure we know where to find him!

"I am the Vine; you are the branches. If someone remains in me and I in them, they will bear much fruit." (St John, chapter 15, verse 5)

What happens if a storm breaks a branch off a fruit tree in an orchard? The crucial flow of sap from trunk to branch is cut off, and the branch dies, unable to produce any more fruit. In Jesus' illustration, he is the trunk, his followers the branches. He wants them to be fruitful, that is, to grow beautiful and attractive Christian characteristics, such as love, patience and self-control; in short, to be like him. For this to happen, they must "remain" in him, that is, closely bound to him, so that the flow of spiritual sap is uninterrupted. Sap is not specifically mentioned or explained, but it's not difficult to find here a link to the Holy Spirit, about whom Jesus has spoken in the previous chapter. This Spirit must keep flowing into Jesus' followers, filling their hearts and minds. Regular prayer, reading the Bible, keeping God's laws and serving other people are just some of the ways of maintaining that flow.

Also important is being with other Christians for mutual support and encouragement, and here is the second layer of meaning behind Jesus' claim to be the Vine. Have you ever ripped up an unwanted book by tearing the pages in half one by one?

It's quite easy. Now try tearing up several pages at once. The pages resist! Solo they fall, together they stand. Jesus knew this vital principle: his followers, left on their own, would be exposed and vulnerable; they would need each other - for mutual support and protection. So Jesus planned that, after his resurrection, his followers would meet together and form local communities. He called it his Church. He is the trunk or stock, his followers grafted in as the branches. They are a unit or 'community'. Firmly linked with him, and together offering mutual protection from cold winds, the branches can be 'fruitful'.

So a Christian is not someone who comes to Jesus just on a one-to-one basis, vital though that is, and then goes it alone. Being an active part of a local church will be important. Yes, I know the Church has many faults, so don't look for the perfect one – it doesn't exist!

St Paul's, Leamington Spa Congregation in 1984

Key word: REMAIN A Christian is someone who, having come to Jesus, seeks to REMAIN in him, along with fellow

Christians, together with them worshiping, learning, caring and serving. Those corporate activities are in themselves crucial conduits through which the Holy Spirit retains a vital presence in the Christian's life.

Key truth: Through the life of a local church, Jesus can rescue us from loneliness and isolation, offering us a 'family' through our fellow Christians, in reality an international family with millions of members the world over!

For further thought: the Holy Spirit - who is he, and what does he do?

Who or what is this 'Holy Spirit'? Earlier on, we mentioned the Trinity, that is the Godhead perceived or experienced in three possible ways, the Holy Spirit taking the role of Life-giver, or In-dweller. At the risk of getting a bit technical, we need once again to look at what the Trinity was 'doing' after the momentous events of Easter. Following his resurrection, Jesus the Son appeared many times to his followers over a period of weeks, confirming to them that he really was alive. This season of appearances came to a decisive end at the event Christians call the Ascension. St Luke records this at the end of chapter 24 of his Gospel, and also in his Book of the Acts, chapter 1, verses 9-11. The message to the disciples is unmistakable. Jesus is leaving the earth to return to his Father's side in heaven. They would not see him again in any kind of bodily form until his return in glory. So how will they manage without his counsel, without the reassurance and comfort of his presence? The answer is: Jesus will send the perfect replacement, the Holy

Spirit. To put it rather crudely, the second and third Persons of the Trinity will swop places!

Before his death, Jesus had clearly explained this to his friends: "I will ask the Father, and he will give you another Counsellor to be with you for ever, the Spirit of truth. All this I have spoken while still with you, but the Counsellor, the Holy Spirit, who the Father will send in my name, will teach you all things." (St John, chapter 14, verses 16-17,25-26) In other words, until Jesus' return, the Holy Spirit would be to all Jesus' followers universally what he had been for three years to his followers locally: teacher, guide, leader, comforter, inspiration and more. What a crucial in-dweller! The sap must flow unhindered!

The parts of the Bible that follow St Luke's Gospel and the Acts, that is the letters of St Paul and other early Christian leaders, spell out more clearly the Holy Spirit's twofold mission. He (and it is 'he', not 'it') is fully God, and not merely an impersonal force. He will firstly enable Christians to become more Christlike, and secondly equip them to serve Christ in the Church and in the world.

Take each in turn. Jesus had spoken of the branches bearing fruit, and St Paul in one of his letters enlarges that image. The 'apples, pears, and oranges' of Christian character to be cultivated in the lives of Christians are love, joy, peace, patience, kindness, goodness, faithfulness, gentleness and self-control. A lovely nine fruits cocktail? No, not quite: in reality, just one fruit, singular, a unified personality, nothing more or less than the reflection of Jesus himself! (St Paul's letter to the Galatians, chapter 5, verses 22-23)

A seemingly impossible task? I have lived in Stratford-upon-Avon in the UK, and sometimes went to the world-famous theatre to see a Shakespeare play. Ask me to write something similar, something as brilliant? I could not possibly do it unless... unless the genius of Shakespeare came to indwell me. Ask me to model the life of Jesus? Impossible, unless his genius, his Spirit, fills, and refills, and refills me, every day.

If the Holy Spirit's first task is to grow his fruit in the lives of believers, his second is to give his gifts to Christians. Fruit, then gifts. We must not confuse the two. Fruit is about character, and there is no opt-out clause. Gifts concern talents or abilities, and no one has them all. Imagine the Christian church, local or wider, as a kind of toolbox, into which the Holy Spirit places a selection of 'tools', as varied as any domestic set. Each tool has a specific and unique role, but all are employed to a common purpose, the 'construction' of the Kingdom of God on earth. So the Holy Spirit distributes, as he pleases, different gifts or abilities around a church's membership. Scattered around the books of the New Testament are six lists of these 'gifts of the Spirit', twenty- seven in all, but the inventory is by no means exhaustive.

As well as some more 'specialist' ones, such as the gift of prophecy, the 'tools' include the ability to preach and teach, skill in administration, the knack of encouraging, the gift of healing, and that servant-heartedness that's always willing to 'get stuck in'; everything in fact that a local church will need to carry out its Jesus-sponsored mission to the world around. Every single member of any church will have been given at least one gift or talent, and because no one has them all, there is no room for boasting or one-upmanship; just like a football eleven, it's team work from start to finish. The challenge for every church member is to discover by prayer, and with the help of their leaders and some experimentation, what gift or gifts the Spirit has given them, and how to develop them to God's glory.

I've heard of 'Holy-Spirit filled Christians'. Are they an elite group in some kind of ecclesiastical Premier League?

They shouldn't be! The Bible commands every Christian believer to "go on being filled with the Spirit." (St Paul's letter to the Ephesians, chapter 5, verse 18) In other words, the Holy Spirit is emphatically not an optional extra for the super deluxe model. People can get confused if they ask the wrong question, along the lines of "how much of the Holy Spirit have I got?" That suggests that the Holy Spirit is like alcoholic spirit - in a bottle for us to drink! A more helpful question is: "how much of me has the Holy Spirit got?" Have I allowed him access to every part of my life, or are there some no-go areas he cannot penetrate? Imagine that your life is like an empty glove, with each of the five fingers representing an important aspect: the thumb standing for work, the second finger for relationships, the third for inmost thoughts, sex life, spending habits, and so on. Now think of the Holy Spirit as like a strong but tender hand, gradually finding its way into the glove. Has that hand filled the thumb, or the first finger, or are the areas of life they stand for barred to the influence and control of Jesus?

When all five fingers have been occupied by the hand, you could say that the glove's owner is "being filled with the Spirit".

A famous Christian leader was once asked if he was filled with the Holy Spirit. "Yes," he replied, "but I leak." (!) It's back to Jesus' command to his branches: "Remain in me…" (St John, chapter 15, verse 4); a daily challenge.

So we have looked at Jesus' "I am" claims, as recorded by St John, and we have noted the possible reason for Jesus choosing seven; but there is one more "I am" utterance in St John's writings, and this is in a league of its own. It occurs in the last book of the Bible, known as Revelation, in which John records not the teaching ministry of Jesus as an itinerant preacher from Galilee, but the proclamations of Jesus Christ the Lord from his throne in heaven. This is what he announces: **"I am the Alpha and the Omega, the First and the Last, the Beginning and the End."** (Revelation, chapter 22, verse 13)

No homely metaphor here, such as bread or gate or shepherd, but a declaration of cosmic supremacy and triumph! Jesus is the universe's A to Z; everything started with him, and will climax in him; he is the 'bookends' of history. This momentous claim is entirely in keeping with him being the second Person, or Son, within the Trinitarian Godhead, and so enjoying a pre- existent state long before his appearance on earth. As one observer has put it, "There was never a time when God was, and Jesus wasn't."

Viewing Jesus Christ on such a vast canvas can profoundly change our perspective on the world around us. Having become a Christian, the Russian author, Leo Tolstoy, wrote: "Jesus Christ changed the stars from being a grim reminder of my insignificance into wondrous monuments of his glory, and my future."

Jesus Christ's claim to be "the End" lends weight to promises he made to his followers whilst with them on earth: although he will definitely leave them (which happened at that event called the Ascension some weeks after his resurrection), he will one day return in glory to gather up his followers, and inaugurate his universal Kingdom of righteousness and peace. Christians call this climax, or winding up of history, the 'Second Coming'. It will be very different from his first coming! Not this time a scarcely noticed little baby, but the unmissable arrival of a majestic Saviour, and at any time, suddenly and unannounced.

Lots of religious cranks have predicted when the world will end, and all got it wrong.

They should look at the Bible! Jesus made it abundantly clear that one Person, and one Person only, knows the time of his return: his Father God. Even Jesus himself, the Son, doesn't know! "No one knows about that day or hour," he said, "not even the angels in heaven, nor the Son, but only the Father." (St Matthew, chapter 24, verse 36) Jesus went on to teach his followers not to speculate about when it would happen, but to spend their energy preparing themselves to meet him. "Stay alert," he said, not to ward off physical viruses, but spiritual or moral infections, and so to be ready for his coming.

Conclusion

L et's summarise: seven (or was it eight in the end!?) great claims from Jesus, all validated later by his resurrection! Three of them, however, were backed up at the time by Jesus performing a miracle, as a sign or visual aid. So immediately before claiming to be the Bread of Life, who satisfies the spiritually hungry, Jesus had satisfied the physically hungry. Taking just five loaves and two fishes, he used his divine power to multiply those meagre provisions into sufficient food to feed a crowd of five thousand. (St John, chapter 6, verses 1-13)

Similarly, his claim to be the Light of the World, offering spiritual insight, was swiftly followed by his miraculous gift of physical sight to a blind man. A truly divine miracle here: the man had been born blind! (St John, chapter 9, verses 1-7) Perhaps, most spectacularly, as Jesus claimed to be the Resurrection and the Life, the Deliverer from our raw mortality, he demonstrated this by bringing back to life a man called Lazarus, who had recently died and been buried. (St John, chapter 11)

These three uniquely powerful miracles have one thing in

common: they could only have been done by God himself, God on earth in human form, in the person of Jesus; and that is precisely the verdict on Jesus John longs his readers to reach. (St John, chapter 20, verses 30-31)

Seven or eight great claims by Jesus; and we can't help noticing one thing the seven had in common? They added up to a multi-faceted rescue package! The Bible has a word for this: **salvation.** It's one of its mega themes - how God wants to **save** us from a host of destructive evil influences. It explains why on the very first Christmas day, the angels announcing Jesus' birth to the shepherds said, "Today in Bethlehem a **Saviour** has been born to you." (St Luke, chapter 2, verse 11)

Good news indeed! But a word of caution: Jesus the Saviour does not simply drop these salvation gifts into our laps! They are not unconditional, and this brings us back to that very first word he said: **repent,** another of the Bible's mega themes.

What is repentance? It is certainly about owning up to our failings and wrongdoing before God, but it is far, far more than simply saying a hasty "Sorry". The word 'repent' has the force of coming to one's senses, stopping, and thinking it out again. In practice? A complete change of attitude. Taking personal responsibility for what is wrong in our lives, and actively turning away from the sins we already know about, let alone those God may reveal to us later! This is hard. The Christian writer CS Lewis called repentance "undergoing a kind of death" - but when God sees someone take just the first step of repentance, his heart is moved, and he comes more than half way to meet them. (Read St Luke, chapter 15, verses 11-32)

That in turn leads more readily to the believing in, and coming to Jesus mentioned earlier.

What next? If this book has ignited a spark of interest in Christianity, here are some ways of fanning that spark into a flame of Christian faith and commitment:

Talk to someone you know and respect who is a definite Christian. Ask them about the difference Jesus makes in their lives, how he has "rescued" them.

Read, or re-read, the Bible in a modern translation. Best not to open at the first page and plod right through. Begin with St Mark's Gospel, the shortest and simplest. Then try St John.

Check out some Christian websites, such as www.bethinking.org.

Tell God that you really want to find him. You could pray something like this: "Dear God, if you exist, please show me who you are, and what you are like. Help me to find Jesus more real and relevant. I genuinely want to know more about you and him, and I am willing to follow through whatever I discover."

Find a church near you that runs sessions for those enquiring about Christianity, and where you can ask all those difficult questions! Look for course brand names such as 'Alpha', 'Christianity Explored', 'Emmaus'.

I think I am too old now to change, it's too late for me to 'get religion.'

Let me say it as strongly as I can: God never sees it that way. "Better late than never," he says; and by way of proof, the Bible records the story of the thief crucified alongside Jesus on Good Friday, who in genuine sorrow for his errors, cast himself on Jesus' mercy, and found it. (St Luke, chapter 23, verses 39-43)

I'm reminded of Alfred Nobel, of Peace Prize fame. A Swedish industrialist, and chemical engineer, Nobel invented dynamite and ballistite, tools of war responsible for many deaths in his lifetime. When his brother died in France, a French newspaper jumped to the conclusion that Alfred was the deceased, and published a damning indictment of his life as the source of such misery and death. So upset was Nobel reading this that he decided to make amends by dedicating his enormous personal fortune to the provision of prizes, for the development of chemistry, physics, medicine, literature - and from 1901, peace! It's never too late to change!

Some Christians are very odd people; I don't want to turn into a Jesus freak.

As we said in the section "I am the Vine", a Christian is someone who has joined Jesus' worldwide 'family', so all Christians everywhere are our 'brothers and sisters'. Now just as you and I cannot pick and choose our earthly relatives, neither can we choose our Christian ones! So our local church will be the place where we rub shoulders with the eccentric, the irritating, the demanding, and the totally challenging, as well as the utterly magnetic and saintly; and as we learn to love and serve them all, some of our own rough edges will be smoothed away. Who knows, we might even become more truly human, more Jesus-like, not so much an aberration but an inspiration! Just six weeks after giving her life to Christ, a member of my church said to me: "My attitude to people is changing. I find that now I come half way to meet them, even the whole way. I am far less critical."

The author with Ugandan clergy - the Christian Church is a huge worldwide international family

So perhaps after reading 'Christianity Unwrapped' you feel ready to take the plunge, and become a Christian, a Christ-in! Here is a prayer you could say that includes repentance, belief, coming, and following. Don't be afraid of saying a prayer like this more than once, several times perhaps, to make sure! God won't get bored - he'll be rejoicing! Read St Luke, chapter 15, verses 7 & 10)

A prayer to receive Christ:

"God, I confess I have sinned against you in my thoughts, words and actions. There are so many good things I have not done. There are so many wrong things I have done – and many of them were completely my fault. I repent of my wrongdoings, and with your help turn from everything I know to be wrong.

I believe that you sent Jesus Christ to die upon the cross to take away my sin. I believe that because of him, you will forgive all my sins, and no longer hold them against me. Thank you so much for showing me your amazing love in this way.

I come to you through Jesus, receiving his light and love, and inviting him, by his Holy Spirit, to enter into my heart, and mind, and will. I want to be in-him, and he in-me for ever. I promise by the power of the Holy Spirit to try to follow him loyally to the end of my life, whatever the cost. AMEN."

If you've just said this prayer, tell someone, another Christian perhaps, as soon as you can. It will help you follow through your commitment to Jesus.

Appendix

Some Explanatory Notes, Extra Bible References, and Questions for Discussion to Supplement the Text.

The epigraph at the beginning of this book is a C.S. Lewis quotation. What is it about Christianity that makes it of 'infinite importance'? Do you agree with Lewis' evaluation?

Page 1: The four lines in italics. Can you think of historical examples of 'religions, philosophies and "isms" that have had their heyday, only then to wane into obscurity? Why did that terminal decline occur? What did they lack to meet human need and aspirations?

Page 2: What do you make of the assertion that even the atheist has to exercise a measure of faith to remain an atheist?

Page 3: Creation, conscience, and the 'Jesus phenomenon' – three areas where to remain an atheist, he or she has to 'believe' the 'unbelievable'. What do you make of these lines of argument? Do you find them convincing?

Pages 4-5: The God of the Old Testament. Read the Hosea & Isaiah verses given in brackets. You could also look up Isaiah 40, verse 11. How do these verses overthrow popular ideas about the God of the Old Testament? What important message do they have for today?

Page 5: Jesus, the much-vaunted man of love, speaking of the reality of Hell. Look up St Mark, chapter 9, verses 42-48; St Matthew, chapter 13, verses 47-50, and chapter 25, verses 31-46; and St Luke, chapter 16, verses 19-31. Did Jesus take pleasure in teaching these realities? See St Luke, chapter 19, verses 41-44.

Why should we take this teaching seriously when so many regard it as medieval superstition?

Page 5: Jesus' description of God as a 'Father'. Do you empathise with the objector's problem, and if so, how can this difficulty be overcome?

Page 6: What do you make of Stephen Hawkins' viewpoint?

Page 6: What is your reaction to the strong contrast between the Christian and Muslim view of God?

Page 8: How convincing do you find the arguments put forward for trusting the four gospels' accounts of the life of Jesus of Nazareth?

Page 9: The Trinity revealing the Godhead as a 'community', influencing Christianity's embracing of a 'we and us' culture. How far has Western individualism dominated our understanding of the Christian Faith? Has it distorted authentic Christianity? If so, what should Christians and the Church do to restore more of a corporate or community ethos?

Pages 9-10: The Trinity. Do the orchestra and H2O illustrations make the concept easier to understand? Are there other illustrations that can shed some light? For an interesting confirmation that the Bible teaches the concept of the Trinity without actually mentioning the word, look up St John, chapter 14, verses 15-17, and chapter 16, verses 5-11. How many divine 'persons' are involved in Jesus' little dialogues? When Jesus was baptised (St Mark, chapter 1, verses 9-11), how many divine 'characters' take part in the drama, and what are their names? You could also look up the first letter of St Peter, chapter 1, verse 2.

Pages 10-11: The Christmas story. What, if anything, has struck you about the Christmas story up until now? Does this page add any new perspective for you? As well as St Paul's second letter to the Corinthians, chapter 8, verse 9, look up Philippians chapter 2, verses 5-11. How do these passages fill out the wonder of the incarnation?

Pages 11-12: The consequences of scientific atheistic humanism. It might be worth pointing out that Hitler, Stalin, Chairman Mao, and Cambodia's Pol Pot, responsible for millions of deaths between them, were all convinced atheists.

Page 13: Grace. Why is the grace of God, or his unmerited mercy, such an important part of the Christian message? What does it prevent? See Ephesians, chapter 2, verses 4-9.

Page 15: All Different. A 20th century example of Christians leading the way in compassion: the first ward dedicated solely to patients with HIV-Aids was in a Christian Mission Hospital in London. Christians have also been prime movers in the more recent Food Bank movement.

Page 16: Jesus in tears. What does this tell us about him? Have a look at the story of Jesus and Lazarus in St John, chapter 11, verses 1-44. What do verses 33, 35, and 38 combine to say? (The verb translated "deeply moved" is incredibly strong in its original Greek form, such that one commentator writes "Jesus approached the grave of Lazarus, in a state, not of uncontrollable grief, but of irrepressible anger. The emotion which tore his breast and clamoured for utterance was just rage". Rage at the grip of death on humankind.

Should Christians believe that Jesus, even in his heavenly glory, still sheds tears of outrage today at his Church's failures, and the world's suffering and injustice? Have a look at Hebrews, chapter 13, verse 8, and chapter 7, verse 25. What do these two verses taken together tell us?

In October 1966, a coal spoil tip in the Welsh village of Aberfan collapsed, killing one hundred and sixteen children in the ruins of their school. A grief-stricken parent shouted at the local priest, "So where is your God now?" The priest replied, "He is buried under there, with the children." How do we react to this?

Pages 16-17: Forgiveness. It's vital to grasp that Christian forgiveness is **not** all about feeling good about the person who has hurt or wronged us, nor even liking them. Have a look at the little scenario described in Exodus, chapter 23, verses 4-5. What would the practical, Mandela-like evidence be that the wronged person had forgiven his enemy or the one who hated him? What light does Romans, chapter 12, verses 19-20 shed on the true meaning of forgiveness?

Pages 18-21: Our anonymous objector raises seven objections to the idea that he or she is a sinner, guilty before God, and so needing rescue. How convincing do you find the answers offered in reply? Can you think of other arguments that people use to try to wriggle out of their culpability before God?

Pages 19-20: Sin – what it really is. Did you gather any fresh perspective from the definitions given? How do Isaiah, chapter 53, verse 6; and Romans, chapter 3, verse 23; and the first letter of St John, chapter 3, verse 4 build up our understanding of the true nature of sin?

An illustration: you are making scrambled eggs, and so break six eggs into a bowl. As the last one goes in, its smell tells you that it is bad. Five are good, but can you still use the mixture? And therefore, when it comes to the mixture of good and bad in us.......?

Pages 26-27: CHRISTIAN – A CHRIST IN: How helpful did you find this attempt to define "Christian"? Could you offer an alternative definition which doesn't make the sort of errors mentioned on page 26?

Page 29: The Kingdom of God. If you do not consider yourself to be a signed-up Christian believer just yet, can you nevertheless identify at all with the concept of God's rule, or presence, beginning to filter into your life? If so, how has this happened? In what kind of ways? Has it begun to bring about some changes?

* * * * *

Pages 30-59: The Seven "I am..." sayings of St John's Gospel

1 Pages 30-32: **"I am the Bread of Life".** Jesus' Feeding of the Five Thousand is the miracle that precedes this claim. Look up St John, chapter 6, verses 1-13. It is the only miracle of Jesus that is recorded in all four gospels, an indication of its huge significance, and – in passing – a pointer to its factual basis. The other references are: St Matthew, chapter 14, verses 13-21; St Mark, chapter 6, verses 30-44; and St Luke, chapter 9, verses 10-17.

The traditional sceptic's view of this incident is that someone in the crowd began to share their picnic with those sitting near to them, and that this act of generosity prompted everyone else to do the same! But what is it about the way the stories are told, and the little details recorded, that strongly militates against this view?

What do you make of the fact that the four accounts differ slightly in some details? Is this a point in their favour, or against them?

If we are to believe that this event really took place, what does this compel us to believe about Jesus' true identity?

Pages 31-32: Holy Communion. What is your experience, if any, of this practice, so important to all Christian churches

77

everywhere in the world? Some people, for reasons they often find it difficult to articulate, recoil from taking part. Why do you think this is so? What kind of help could we offer them?

Did you find the illustration of the wedding ring (page 33) helpful or inadequate?

2 Pages 33-35: **"I am the Light of the World".** This claim of Jesus is followed by his healing of the man born blind, which powerfully illustrates the true significance of the claim. Look up St John, chapter 9, verses 1-41.

What vital truth about suffering does this story convey? (verse 3)

In what ways (plural!) did the man begin to see? (verse 7, 11, 17, 25, 33, 38)

Who were the really blind in the story? (verse 34, 40, 41)

Jesus stresses the need to "follow" him, in order to benefit from his light. What does it mean to "follow" Jesus?

Page 35: Born again. What sort of image is conjured up in your mind when you hear this phrase? Why did Jesus tell the respectable and religious Nicodemus (St John, chapter 3, verses 1-16) that he had to be born again? Why do living a moral life, and being religious fall short of bringing people into the Kingdom of God? (verse 3, 5)

If you know that you have definitely been born again into God's Kingdom, can you describe what happened? How it happened? In what ways has it brought you into a new "light" that you didn't know before?

What do you make of the university professor's honest confession? (page 37)

3 Pages 38-41: **"I am the Gate for the Sheep".** Look up St John, chapter 10, verses 7-10. If idolatrous paganism and the seductive lure of the occult were the main hostile forces threatening the Jewish people's relationship with God, what forces constitute the main threat to the faith and commitment of Christians today? See the first letter of Peter, chapter 2, verse 1, 11. How can Jesus act as a protective "fold" in which to take refuge? Why does Peter describe Christians as "aliens and strangers in the world"? St James, chapter 4, verse 4 says that "friendship with the world is hatred towards God." What does he mean by "friendship with the world", and how do we avoid this whilst at the same time showing Christian love towards all we meet?

Pages 39-41 : Leadership. What does Jesus teach in St Mark, chapter 9, verses 33-37; and chapter 10, verses 41-45? See also the first letter of Peter, chapter 5, verses 2-3. What challenges are there here for all would-be leaders, and especially those in the Church?

The Bible does not comment only on spiritual or church leadership. It has things to say to secular leaders. See Proverbs, chapter 12, verse 15; chapter 14, verse 16; chapter 15, verses 31-32; chapter 16, verses 10, 13, 18; chapter 19, verse 6; chapter 19, verse 17; chapter 20, verse 26; chapter 28, verse 3; chapter 29, verse 4, 12; chapter 31, verses 4-5, 8-9.

4 Pages 43-44: **"I am the Good Shepherd".** See St John, chapter 10, verses 11-18. On a superficial reading, the Easter story portrays Jesus as a helpless victim of rank injustice and cruelty, but what is Jesus' own perspective? (verses 17-18) Why is this perspective important?

What impresses you most about the events of Good Friday? (pages 44-46)

Some critics of Christianity find its emphasis on the cross as offensive. Why is this? See the first letter of Paul to the Corinthians, chapter 1, verses 18-25. How can someone's drawn out, public execution possibly be the "power" and "wisdom" of God?

Hebrews, chapter 9, verse 22 sums up the teaching of the entire Bible, that there can be no re-entry for sinners into the presence of a holy God without blood sacrifice. Why is this a non-negotiable truth? (See Romans, chapter 6, verse 23 taken together with Leviticus, chapter 17, verse 11)

5 Pages 50-54: "**I am the Resurrection and the Life**".

How convinced are you by the circumstantial evidence for the resurrection? Is there one particular piece of evidence that especially strikes you? If you remain unconvinced, can you pinpoint where your doubts lie?

Page 54: How easy do you find it to make the jump from accepting that Jesus' resurrection happened, to believing that it was, or is, a "cosmic event in which we can share"?

6 Pages 55-57: "**I am the Way, the Truth, and the Life.**" How convinced are you of the uniqueness of Jesus, compared with all other religious leaders? How useful are the American story, and illustrations of the key, and meeting a long lost friend?

7 Pages 58-60: **"I am the Vine".** Jesus' claim leads on to the age-old question: can you be a Christian and not go to church? What do you think? What did John Wesley mean when he said, "To turn Christianity into a solitary religion is to destroy it".

Look up Paul's first letter to the Corinthians, chapter 12, verses 12-20, 27. What illustration does Paul use to make a similar point to Jesus' teaching on the vine and branches?

If you have had a seriously unfortunate experience of church but are still connected and involved, what was it that kept you "hanging in" there?

Pages 60-62: The Holy Spirit: For more on the fruit of Christian character, see Ephesians, chapter 4, verse 25 through to chapter 5, verse 7. For examples of the Spirit's gifts, or tools, see Romans, chapter 12, verses 3-8; Paul's first letter to the Corinthians, chapter 12, verses 7-11, 28-31; Ephesians, chapter 4, verses 7-13; and the first letter of Peter, chapter 4, verses 10-11.

If you were to use the glove illustration,(page 63) what significant areas of your life would you assign to each of the five fingers?

8 Page 64: **"I am the Alpha and the Omega, the First and the Last."** Jesus had claimed something similar during his earthly ministry. See St John, chapter 8, verses 57-58. What difference does it make to your worldview and perspective on life to see Jesus as "the bookends of history"? Can you identify with Tolstoy?

Jesus' promise to return in glory. For a fuller description of this event, see the first letter of Paul to the Thessalonians, chapter 4, verses 13-18. How should this affect our daily lives? See St Matthew, chapter 24, verses 36-44; and the first letter of John, chapter 3, verses 2-3.

* * * * *

Page 67: Salvation. What excites you or moves you most about this promised gift from God?

On the first Christmas night, the angels did **not** say to the shepherds, "Today the mother of all teachers has been born to you….." or "the most perfect human example has been born to you…." or "the most inspiring leader has been born to you…..", although all three of those would have been true! Instead the angels' message was, "a **Saviour** has been born to you…" What is so special and important about this word?

Repentance: As we saw on page 29, "repent" was one of the very first commands Jesus gave when he started his public ministry. Other parts of the Bible back up the importance of repentance. See St Luke, chapter 24, verses 46-47; Acts chapter 2, verse 38; chapter 17, verse 30-31; chapter 26, verse 20; Romans chapter 2, verse 5.

Page 67: How does CS Lewis' description of repentance as "undergoing a kind of death" strike you? What encouragements are there for the truly penitent? See St Luke, chapter 15, verses 7,10, 11-24.

Page 69: "Some Christians put me off…..!" There is a cost

to identifying with Jesus Christ, and by association, with his followers. What does Jesus teach about this in St Matthew, chapter 10, verses 32-33, and St Mark, chapter 8, verse 38?

Page 71: The prayer to receive, or come, to Christ. How do we know that Christ will accept us? Look up St John, chapter 6, verse 37; and Revelation, chapter 3, verse 20. Here the risen Christ is speaking to people who, realising their spiritual poverty, are willing to repent and believe. What is "the door" outside of which he patiently stands? What promise does he make to those on the other side?

About the Author

Born in 1946, Andrew Dow came to faith in Christ through a Boys' Bible Class in his Hertfordshire home town. After studying theology at university, he spent two years teaching in Uganda, before training for ordination into the ministry of the Church of England. Ordained in 1971, he served as the vicar of churches in Leamington Spa, Solihull, Bristol, and Cheltenham before retiring in 2010 to the West Midlands. He continues to preach and lead services occasionally, with the constant support of his wife, Miriam, and their two daughters, Jennie and Carrie.

A keen railway enthusiast like so many clergy, Andrew has a model railway; and he plays the trumpet in a local orchestra. He is also a competent amateur photographer, and has taken official pictures for three local Neighbourhood Development Plans. He has his own website: AJMD Photography URL: https://dow4519.picfair.com, where you can view (and even buy!) some of his better shots.

Printed in Great Britain
by Amazon